MY TODDLER
RULES THE HOUSE

Paul & Karen Tautges

Consulting Editor: Dr. Paul Tautges

Help! My Toddler Rules the House

© 2010 by Paul & Karen Tautges

ISBN
Paper: 978-1-63342-009-0
ePub: 978-1-63342-010-6
Kindle: 978-1-63342-011-3

Published by **Shepherd Press**
P.O. Box 24
Wapwallopen, PA 18660

www.shepherdpress.com

All Scripture quotations, unless stated otherwise, are from the New American Standard Bible, The Lockman Foundation, 1995.

First printed by Day One Publications

Designed by **documen**

CONTENTS

INTRODUCTION

"**We** just can't take it anymore. We're ready to take our son to a psychiatrist!" exclaimed Caleb as his wife, Susie, nodded in utter exhaustion.[1] These newcomers to our church had come to visit my wife and me at our house on a Tuesday evening because they said they needed "family counseling." It turned out that their three-year-old son's behavior had brought them to the end of themselves. He was ruling their house. As they sat on our living-room sofa we listened. We then began explaining to them the biblical principles of child-rearing, the priority of a child's obedience, and the means of correction prescribed in God's Word, the Bible. After they agreed to consistently apply what we had taught them, we prayed and they went home.

Two Sundays later, Caleb and Susie approached us in the foyer of our church meeting place and declared, "We have a different son!" Caleb described the changes they were observing in their son's attitude and behavior since they began to faithfully apply the biblical principles we had taught them. They had begun to receive the Bible as the revelation of God and, therefore, authoritative for their family. And they were already seeing a difference its application was making in their home.

We assume you have picked up this booklet because either someone you know or you yourself also face the challenge of raising children in a fallen world and are in need of some help. It contains the foundational counsel that we have given to many couples like Caleb and Susie over the years. We trust and pray you will find the help you seek as well as encouragement from the practical counsel contained in its pages.

1

Sad Results of Child-Centered Parenting

We live in a society dominated by child-centered parenting. A typical walk through a shopping mall or local grocery store often reveals this sad truth. The frequent occurrence of temper tantrums from children leads the discerning person to ask, "Just who is in charge anyway?" The authors of this booklet are not the only ones concerned about this epidemic. Several years ago our local newspaper dedicated almost ¼ of a page to printing an Associated Press article: "Please, Please, Please? Nagging Has Become Norm for Many Youth."[2] The purpose of the article was to comment on the results of a survey commissioned by the Center for a New American Dream, which "promotes responsible consumption of resources and goods." In other words, the center is upset by the power that advertisers have over young minds and hopes to "persuade Congress to pass laws further limiting advertising to young people." Is this really the answer? Do we need more laws governing the advertising industry? Isn't that like putting a self-stick bandage over a broken bone? Could there be a better solution? Could it be that the best answer is to return to one of the essential building blocks of common-sense parenting—divinely delegated authority?

We are not suggesting that every parent must believe his or her authority is from God in order to be a "good parent" in the eyes of society. We only expect that from Christians. However, it seems that, deep down, every conscience is at least remotely bothered by the idea of children ruling their parents. What is so desperately needed today is teaching geared toward parents that will help them realize that God has delegated a portion of his authority to them for the well-being of their children and that they don't have to apologize for using it. Of course, they must also not abuse it, but nowadays almost anything that interferes with a child's happiness is somehow twisted into a portrayal of "abuse."

Today's parents desperately need to be taught that the most loving thing they can do for their children is to be in charge. Parents must be taught to just say "No." Even Betsy Taylor, executive director of the above-mentioned center based in the state of Maryland recognizes this: "Ultimately," she says, "it's a parent's responsibility to set better limits and stick to them." "When it comes to nagging," the article states, 55 percent of the youth surveyed said they can "usually get their parents to give in." Additionally, 60 percent admitted they could "manipulate their parents on 'small things' before they started first grade." Marian Salzman, the chief strategic officer for an ad agency, admitted that "kids are at the center of today's households." She's dead right.

The polled youth were between the ages of twelve and seventeen, however, "experts say nagging is a habit learned much earlier." I am reluctant to admit it, but for once the experts are right. The embarrassing results of child-centered parenting do not begin to show themselves in the clothing store at twelve or thirteen years old. They start at a much younger age. In fact, they begin before the crib is disassembled and hauled up to the attic. For the child-centered parent, the world revolves around that little bundle of joy. Child-centered parents reason, "We can't go here because it may interrupt little Bobby's naptime." "We can't go there because little Sally won't like the food." "If we do that then Joey may fuss." "If we go out tonight then Julie will give the babysitter a hard time." And on and on it goes. It seems that every time junior cries, a new family crisis has begun.

Conversely, fathers and mothers who truly love their children are not the ones guilty of this epidemic of indulgence. It is those who think they love their children, but in reality love themselves far more, who are at fault. What do we mean? True love always looks toward the long-term best of the person being loved. That means it is more loving to tell a person truth that hurts than to silently watch him or her self-destruct. It means it is more loving to discipline your children so that they refrain from playing in the street than to let them get run over by a car. It means it is more loving to say "No" to greedy little children in order to prepare them to live in an unfriendly world where everything will not always go their own way. Wise parents realize this and do not use their children as personal security blankets, but steadfastly endure temporary inconveniences (like disciplining for temper tantrums) because they rightly believe that in the end their children will love them for it.

Sadly, however, this is no longer considered *normal* parenting. The survey mentioned above found that, "even when their parents say 'no,' nearly six of 10 young people keep nagging—an average of nine times." The same survey "found that 10 percent of 12 and 13-year-olds said they ask their parents more than 50 times for products they've seen advertised." Experts call it the "nag factor." And marketing agencies continue to bank on it. It is estimated the "nag factor" will be responsible for influencing a projected $40 billion of spending for children aged four to twelve in 2010. That's a high price to pay for lazy parenting. But what does the Scripture say? Does God's Word provide us with reliable counsel in response to this trend? Yes, it does. In fact, it warns us against child-centered parenting for at least three reasons.

Child-Centered Parenting Leads to the Parents' Shame

When our children witness "shopping mall tantrums," one of them is sure to comment on the shameful behavior. "Daddy, did you see that boy?" "Mommy, did you hear what that girl said to her mother?" When they do this we quickly remind them that they too are sinners who are in need of correction and that if we do not faithfully discipline them, sinful anger will become a pattern in their own lives. By being too lazy to stick to the first, second, or third *No*, we as parents train junior to ask nine times. In other words, though the little child is indeed guilty, at this point the greater shame belongs to us as parents who should know better and should love our child enough to train him or her to act properly. Otherwise, the wise observer may silently ask, "What is wrong with that parent?" This is Proverbs 29:15 in action:

> The rod and reproof give wisdom,
> But a child who gets his own way brings
>   shame to his mother.

Child-Centered Parenting Feeds Self-Destructive Lifestyles

The worst example of child-centered parenting found in the Bible is the sad story of Eli, the priest of Israel. His family's history is a classic example of what happens when a parent respects his or her child too much. It is role reversal of the most embarrassing kind, and for Eli's family the consequences were nothing short of deadly. God's warning came to Eli by the mouth of a man of God who stated that God's chastening hand was about to fall upon the priest and his sons because Eli honored them above God (1 Samuel 2:29). As a result, the strength of his priesthood would be broken (2:31) and both his sons, Hophni and Phinehas, would die tragically on the same day (2:34). What may have been only a few days later, Eli's young servant, Samuel, was awakened from sleep by the voice of God. God explained, "I have told him [Eli] that I am about to judge his house forever for the iniquity which he knew, because his sons brought a curse on themselves and he did not rebuke them" (1 Samuel 3:13).

Shortly thereafter, Israel went into battle against the Philistines and suffered a total loss. Thirty thousand soldiers died, the ark of the covenant was stolen, and Hophni and Phinehas died on the same day—exactly as Samuel had prophesied (4:10–11). What a tragic end! Unfortunately, the consequences did not stop with Eli. It appears that Samuel may have followed Eli's wimpy example, for when his own sons were grown they "did not walk in his ways, but turned aside after dishonest gain and took bribes and perverted justice" (1 Samuel 8:3).

What was the problem? Eli failed to say *No* and mean it. That is, he relinquished his God-given authority to lead his sons in righteousness. When he learned of their shamefully self-indulgent behavior, he did not respond with the degree of gravity warranted by the situation (2:12–17). Instead, he let them rule the house. His correction appears to have been more like a simple slap on his sons' hands while saying, "No, no, no, the people are talking" (2:24). This response is typical of child-centered parents, as they usually do not *command* their children, but *reason* with them instead. They fear their children's response more than they fear God. However, God-centered parenting calls for the firm use of divinely delegated authority for the sake of protecting children from their own foolishness. Jim Newheiser is correct when he writes, "Neglect of discipline is among the worst forms of child abuse."[3]

Child-Centered Parenting Is an Abdication of God-given Authority and Responsibility

King David also reaped the torrential downpour of pain that often comes as a result of child-centered parenting. On his deathbed he received word that his son Adonijah had "exalted himself, saying, 'I will be king.' So he prepared for himself chariots and horsemen with fifty men to run before him" (1 Kings 1:5). We would be forced to wonder what led to this behavior if the Holy Spirit had not so graciously given us the very next verse: "His father had never crossed him at any time by asking, 'Why have you done so?'" (1:6). Adonijah was another sad product of parental indulgence. We do not mean to say his rebellion was entirely the king's fault. David's son was responsible for his own actions. But it is obvious from the text that Adonijah was not given the gift of self-discipline, which usually comes through the tutorial of parental discipline. Faithful correction from parents is one of God's most effective tools for the development of self-control in the hearts of children.

Parents, our God-fearing example is of great importance, but it is not enough. It wasn't for Eli, Samuel, or David. It must be accompanied by a proper exercise of our God-given authority. These tragic examples illustrate the fact that spoiled children often live out their self-indulgence right into adulthood. Parents, please help lower the statistics! Please love your child enough to prepare him or her for a life of self-denial by setting healthy boundaries and firmly maintaining them. Although God has a heart for children, he never intended life to revolve around them. Please say *No* when you must. Please mean *No* when you say it. And please stick to your answer unless wisdom leads you to change it. Love your children, care for them responsibly, train them diligently, but, by all means, do not allow them to become the center of your little universe.

FROM ONE MOM TO ANOTHER

One of our little ones, in particular, loves to ask for things. It may be just a piece of chewing gum from my purse. If I give the answer "You need to wait" and that same child soon asks again, I will usually say, "No. You cannot have the gum now. Mommy said you needed to wait, but you have asked me again." By doing this, I am trying to teach self-control. Sometimes we ask God for things and we have to wait. What better time for us to learn to patiently wait than when we are children? When we grow to be adults and ask God for a new car we will be much better able to handle his answer of "Not now" if we have been learning this valuable lesson our whole lives.

2

Are You Raising a Cain?

Some time ago, while sitting in the doctor's office with one of our children, I (Paul) picked up a pamphlet entitled *Temper Tantrums: A Normal Part of Growing Up*. In it, the American Academy of Pediatrics states, "Parents need to accept that temper tantrums are a result of the child's inner struggles in growing up. They are a normal and expected part of child development."[4] To counsel parents dealing with these outbursts, the academy asserts that spanking is *never* an option. Instead, parents are encouraged to ignore the out-of-control child or do something to distract the child in hopes that he or she will get over his or her fit.

Now we agree with part of that statement. Fits of temper are considered by many to be normal and they certainly are to be expected, but that is because of the sinfulness of the human heart, which manifests its rebellion in a multitude of ways. However, tantrums most definitely cannot be ignored if parents want to do what is best for their children. Parents should not accept that their children simply need time to work through this "stage" of their development while the parents simply "hang on," hoping to survive until this one ends and the next "stage" begins.

Is the academy's counsel acceptable to Christian parents who strive to please God by training their children to fear the Lord and exercise self-control? Does the Bible reveal God's will for parents and their children, and what may happen to those children if we make a habit of letting them get their own way? Does the Bible reveal God's answer for the rebellion inherent in the human heart? Indeed it does.

What Temper Tantrums Reveal about the Child

When the first man and woman, Adam and Eve, rebelled against their Creator's clear and good command, "sin entered into the world, and death through sin, and so death spread to all men, because all sinned" (Romans 5:12). Thus, Adam and Eve's children were the first to inherit a sin nature—an inborn tendency to demand one's own way.

The biblical account of Cain and Abel is well

known. God accepted the offering of Abel and rejected that of Cain. In turn, Cain became angry and murdered his brother. Uncontrolled anger, however, was not Cain's core problem but was the fruit of a more corrupt root. In order to discern his real problem we need to take a look at the four times Cain is described in the Bible.

First, in Genesis 4, we learn that Abel was a shepherd while Cain was a farmer (v. 2). When it came time to bring an offering to the Lord, Abel brought what God required; Cain did not. God's rejection of Cain's offering sent Cain into a fit of anger and subsequent depression (v. 5). Left unbridled, Cain's tantrum led him to become a slave to sin (v. 7), to commit murder (v. 8), and, finally, to lie to God (v. 9).

Second, in Hebrews 11, the "faith chapter," we read that Abel brought "a better sacrifice than Cain" (v. 4), because he brought it in faith and righteousness. However, Cain is not credited with faith or righteousness since he did not regard God's commands as authoritative. He did not trust God enough to walk by faith. His offering was, therefore, unacceptable because it did not meet God's requirement.

Third, in the first letter written by John we learn something of the fuel that fanned the flame of Cain's hatred toward his brother. The apostle John asks, "And for what reason did he [Cain] slay him [Abel]? Because his deeds were evil, and his brother's were righteous" (3:12). Cain so despised God's ways that he sought to destroy anyone who reminded him of God's righteous standards, including his own brother.

Fourth, we find Cain mentioned in the book of Jude, which was written to urge believers to oppose false teachers who were infiltrating churches. In describing these false prophets, Jude indicated that "they have gone the way of Cain" (v. 11). Why did he liken these heretics to Cain? Cain was not a false teacher. A brief look at the context, however, reveals the core problem of both parties. Jude describes them as "ungodly persons who turn the grace of our God into licentiousness and *deny our only Master and Lord,* Jesus Christ" (v. 4); men who "defile the flesh, and *reject authority*" (v. 8); "*without fear,* caring for themselves" (v. 12); and "following after *their own ungodly lusts*" (v. 18).[5]

Clearly, the "way of Cain" is the way of rebellion. It is the way of all those who despise and reject authority. Cain refused to acknowledge that anyone, including God, had any right to control his behavior. He was his own boss. His willful spirit had never been broken and brought to the place of willing submission.

Herein lies the challenge for parents: if we do not lovingly teach our children to respect and obey our authority, our children may in turn grow up to reject other forms of divinely delegated authority and eventually despise God, who is the source of all authority. Children who are not trained to submit to authority figures they *can* see may, apart from a transforming work of God's grace, face a lifelong struggle to submit to the God whom they *cannot* see. Knowing this tendency of sinful human nature, faithful parents will purge stubbornness and defiance from their child's will so that one day the child may say with David, "A broken and a contrite heart, O God, You will not despise" (Psalm 51:17). God's most basic command to children is to honor and obey their parents. When we fail to train our children to obey God— by obeying their parents—we prepare them to live lives of self-centered rebellion, and we are guilty of raising Cains.

What an Absence of Discipline Reveals about the Parent

The primary duty of Christian parents is to take a natural-born fool and cause him or her to be filled with the wisdom of God. Perhaps this statement startles you, but let us explain what we mean by it. Unselfishness in parenting means that we must lay aside our self-interest and love of convenience in order to do what is in the long-term best interests of our children—we *must* discipline them toward respectful obedience. This discipline is not an option for parents who are committed to raising their children to follow the Lord and become responsible members of society. If we choose to neglect the correction of our children, it may reveal two painful realities concerning our own hearts as parents.

» *We do not love our child, but rather we hate him or her.* "He who withholds his rod hates his son, but he who loves him disciplines him diligently" (Proverbs 13:24). Neglect of discipline reveals that we love ourselves more than we love our children.

» *We esteem ourselves more than we esteem our child.* "Do nothing from selfishness or empty conceit, but with humility of mind regard one another as more important than yourselves; do not merely look out for your own personal interests, but also for the interests of others ["others" includes our children]" (Philippians 2:3–4). Faithfulness in the parenting task is one of the obvious ways in which we look out for the long-term interests of our children above our own.

What May Happen to our Child if We Withhold Correction

The Bible also provides ample warning concerning the harmful results of an absence of child discipline.

»   *Our child may choose a sinful lifestyle or become settled into evil habits.* "Discipline your son while there is hope" (Proverbs 19:18). The phrase "while there is hope" implies that if we wait too long, discipline becomes more difficult and we may lose our opportunity to mold our children's characters and direct them to God.

»   *Our child may remain enslaved to foolishness.* "Foolishness is bound up in the heart of a child; the rod of discipline will remove it far from him" (Proverbs 22:15).

»   *Our child may grow up to despise us.* "Fathers, do not provoke your children to anger, but bring them up in the discipline and instruction of the Lord" (Ephesians 6:4).

» *Our child may grow to be self-righteous and arrogant.* "There is a kind of man who curses his father and does not bless his mother. There is a kind who is pure in his own eyes, yet is not washed from his filthiness. There is a kind— oh how lofty are his eyes! And his eyelids are raised in arrogance" (Proverbs 30:11–13).

» *Our child may suffer an early death or we may unintentionally steer him toward hell.* "Do not hold back discipline from the child, although you strike him with the rod, he will not die. You shall strike him with the rod and rescue his soul from Sheol"[6] (Proverbs 23:13–14).

We Are All Like Cain

Though we may not be guilty of taking another person's life by means of murder, we, and our children, are like Cain in that we are guilty of sinning against God and spurning his authority. Consider just four basic ways we all, as sinners, resemble Cain.

» *Each of us has lied to God, others, and perhaps*

even to ourselves. "... [A]s it is written, 'There is none righteous, not even one ... All have turned aside ... There is none who does good, There is not even one. Their throat is an open grave, with their tongues they keep deceiving,' 'The poison of asps is under their lips' " (Romans 3:10–13). "If we say that we have no sin, we are deceiving ourselves and the truth is not in us" (1 John 1:8). *But there is good news in Jesus:* "If we confess our sins, He is faithful and righteous to forgive us our sins and to cleanse us from all unrighteousness" (1 John 1:9).

» *Each of us lacks God's perfect righteousness.* "For all of us have become like one who is unclean, and all our righteous deeds are like a filthy garment; and all of us wither like a leaf, and our iniquities, like the wind, take us away" (Isaiah 64:6). *But there is good news in Jesus:* "For if by the transgression of the one [Adam], death reigned through the one, much more those who receive the abundance of grace and of the gift of righteousness will reign in life through the One, Jesus Christ" (Romans 5:17).

» *Each of us has committed evil against God and against others.* "... [F]or all have sinned and fall short of the glory of God" (Romans 3:23). *But there is good news in Jesus: "... being justified as a gift by His grace through the redemption which is in Christ Jesus"* (Romans 3:24).

» *Each of us has acted independently from God.* "All of us like sheep have gone astray, each of us has turned to his own way" (Isaiah 53:6a). *But there is good news in Jesus: "... But the LORD has caused the iniquity of us all to fall on Him [the Messiah, Jesus Christ]"* (Isaiah 53:6b).

The bad news is that, as did Cain, we have each sinned in Adam. We have despised God's righteous authority by acting independently of him. But the good news is that God sent his only begotten Son into the world to offer his sinless life as the perfect sacrifice for our sins and then be raised from the dead three days later. This is the gospel! Now God commands each of us to repent of our rebellion and to believe in Jesus Christ—to trust him as the Sin-bearer who gave his life on the cross and as the only risen Lord who lives to save us from eternal separation from God.

Only when we embrace these biblical truths concerning ourselves and concerning Jesus will we be able to lead our children to an understanding of the sinfulness of their own hearts and direct them to submit to the overcoming grace of God in the gospel. How about you? Have you been born again by the mercy of God? Are you trusting in Jesus Christ as the only one who can reconcile you to God? If not, call upon him today, for

> Whoever will call on the name of the
> Lord will be saved.
>
> (Romans 10:13)

The responsibilities of parenting are indeed enormous. Though our children's hearts are naturally bound by foolishness, we have the privilege of being involved in the process of imparting God's wisdom to them through our faithful, gospel-driven discipline. Ultimately, we cannot change our children's hearts. Only the Holy Spirit can do that by means of the instruction of God's Word concerning Jesus Christ and his gospel. However, our faithfulness in carrying out our God-given responsibilities prepares our children's hearts to submit to the Lord and to his life-transforming gospel.

FROM ONE MOM TO ANOTHER

In a helpful booklet entitled *Under Loving Command*, fellow mom Pat Fabrizio writes, "My obedience to God to train my child requires that every time I ask him to do something, either 'come here,' 'don't touch,' 'hush,' 'put that down' ... or whatever it is, I must see that he obeys. When I have said it once in a normal tone, if he does not obey immediately, I must take up the switch and spank him (love demands this) enough to hurt so he will not want it repeated."[7]

When I read this it had an enormous impact upon me. I realized I had once again fallen into the habit of repeating my commands several times without even noticing it. Over the years, I've recognized that when I carefully follow through with my directions the first time, I don't risk being out of control because I don't allow myself the opportunity to be angered. Instead, by being consistent in holding my children to the standard of cheerful first-time obedience, I am teaching them that all of life is lived under authority—ultimately the authority of God. My husband is convinced that when we are consistent with this habit it prepares our children to hear the bad news about their sin and to believe the good news about Jesus by obeying his gospel.

3

Cultivating Plants and Directing Arrows

Psalms 127 and 128 contain some of the most precious words concerning God's blessing upon marriage and his gift of children. In these two psalms, the songwriter chooses two simple illustrations that provide instruction for the task of parenting.

Children Are Like Arrows

> Like arrows in the hand of a warrior,
> So are the children of one's youth.
>
> (Psalm 127:4)

Perhaps the writer likens children to arrows for two reasons.

CHILDREN MUST BE CAREFULLY CRAFTED

In Old Testament days archers did not drive to their local sporting goods store to purchase arrows. Instead, they walked to the nearest patch of woods in search of a branch that could be whittled and shaped to suit their intended purpose. In the same way, the character of children is directly shaped by their parents (sometimes even without our conscious awareness). Nevertheless, the power parents have over their children must be used for their children's ultimate good. The New Testament exhortation that corresponds well here is from the apostle Paul's letter to the believers in the city of Ephesus.

> *Fathers, do not provoke your children to anger, but bring them up in the discipline and instruction of the Lord.*
>
> (Ephesians 6:4)

Rather than habitually irritating our children to the point of resentment, we are to diligently train them to love and obey God. The word "discipline" includes education, training, and correction to the standard established in the Christian household.[8] If our goal is to "launch" our arrow-like children forth from our homes as responsible, godly adults we must train them with all diligence, using God-fearing education to carefully craft their characters.

CHILDREN MUST BE PURPOSELY DIRECTED

In addition to instilling God-fearing character into the lives of our children by means of education, we must give clear direction and correction from the Word of God. Because of indwelling sin, children left to themselves do not naturally choose God's ways. They must be purposely directed toward salvation in Christ and to a life of godliness. In Ephesians 6:4 quoted above, Paul uses the word "instruction," which could also be translated "admonition." This refers to training by "the word of encouragement."[9] The purpose of admonition is to warn and to correct so as to instill a proper fear of God in the hearts of our children as we direct them to a life of obedience to him.

> The fear of the LORD is the beginning of knowledge;
> Fools despise wisdom and instruction.
> (Proverbs 1:7)

When verbal admonition is not sufficient to correct a child's foolishness, other forms of reproof may become necessary in order to bring the child's will to a place of submission. This will be fully explained in the next chapter. When biblical instruction and correction are carried out in the atmosphere of godly example they yield blessed results. Thus the arrows in one's quiver are carefully crafted and purposely directed to follow the ways and knowledge of God.

> A righteous man who walks in his
>   integrity—
> How blessed are his sons after him.
>
> (Proverbs 20:7)

Children Are Like Plants

> Your wife shall be like a fruitful vine
> Within your house,
> Your children like olive plants
> Around your table.
>
> (Psalm 128:3)

Perhaps the writer likens children to plants for three reasons.

CHILDREN NEED NOURISHMENT

Resembling tender sprouts, which flourish under the care of a faithful gardener, children blossom when their parents are obedient to God's command to constantly nourish them toward maturity. Tender care is what the phrase "bring them up" in Ephesians 6:4 refers to ("bring them up in the discipline and instruction of the Lord"). Parents are obligated before God to carefully exercise the disciplinary function of love within a home that promotes God's truth—the "instruction of the Lord"—as the only acceptable way to live.

CHILDREN NEED WEEDING

Like young plants, children are prone to be overtaken by weeds—the weeds of sin and foolishness—and, therefore, need their parents to cultivate wisdom by means of correction. Proverbs 22:15 is clear:

> Foolishness is bound up in the heart of
> a child;
> The rod of discipline will remove it far
> from him.

The "rod of discipline" is the God-ordained means of removing foolishness from our children's hearts in order that they may become partakers of divine wisdom. God's wisdom will then bear much more desirable fruits, including purity, peace, gentleness, reasonableness, mercy, stability, and genuineness (James 3:17).

CHILDREN NEED PRUNING

Jesus says in John 15:1–2,

> I am the true vine, and My Father is the
> vinedresser. Every branch in Me that does
> not bear fruit, He takes away; and every
> branch that bears fruit, He prunes it so
> that it may bear more fruit.

Corrective discipline is a demonstration of God's love for his children. In the same way, we as parents must use the pruning process of chastisement to remove dead wood and diseased branches from our children's lives so that they may bear God-honoring fruit. When we nourish, weed, and prune our "family garden," our children grow up to be pleasant and fruitful plants around our table.

FROM ONE MOM TO ANOTHER

One thing I've done with our young children is to consistently establish eye contact with them before giving a command. "Look at my eyes," is what they often hear. Once I have their attention I usually crouch down to their level so that I can talk directly to them. If they are looking into my eyes while I give my instructions, I know they have heard me and I can then hold them accountable. Then, if the instruction is not obeyed, I know without a doubt they have disobeyed and I must carry through with the proper discipline.

This has become especially important over the years since four of our children are hearing-impaired from birth. Because of this genetic weakness it would be easy for them to use "I didn't hear you" as an excuse, or for us to conclude, "I don't think they heard me." By gaining and maintaining eye contact while giving commands we have been able to guard against this common form of excuse-making.

Thankfully, before we knew our oldest son could not hear us, we had already established this routine. By training him to look into our eyes he was also being trained to read our lips. We are so thankful for the wisdom the Lord gave us at the beginning of our parenting experience. "Look at my eyes" developed an unexpected skill and means of communication in our son's life.

4

The Seven Laws of Correction

The book of Proverbs unmistakably calls for the physical discipline of children, that is, spanking, or corporal punishment, as a necessary part of wise and effective parenting. For instance:

> He who withholds his rod hates his son,
> But he who loves him disciplines him
>   diligently.
>
> (13:24)

This verse alone refutes the incorrect thinking of some who conclude, "I love my child too much to spank him." (Different regions have different policies on corporal punishment. While this booklet explains the biblical model of child discipline, parents should be aware of the legal requirements of the country or state in which they reside.)

Parents who truly love their children will do what is necessary to protect them from the pain and destruction caused by the rebelliousness of sin. Clear-headed parents are willing, from the perspective of "future-minded love," to inflict temporal pain upon their children in order to save them not only from the destruction caused by a sinful lifestyle, but, more importantly, from the pain of eternal damnation and separation from God.

One problem facing us today is that some parents, in the past and even in the present, have used spanking improperly and, therefore, their actions may rightly be considered abusive. Certainly there are parents who abuse their children under the guise of "spanking," but that is not what we are talking about in this chapter. When spanking is used to abuse children it is nothing short of wickedness in the sight of God. Like all sin, child abuse is harmful to others and should be opposed. But those in our society who want to classify all spanking as child abuse are simply wrong. They misunderstand what biblical discipline is and how it is to be properly practiced. Therefore, it is our desire to set before you seven steps in the discipline process that help us to consistently put sound principles into action, lovingly, on behalf of our children.

1. Clearly Communicate Your Behavioral Expectations

Just as God makes his standard clear in his Word, so parents should communicate their expectations to their children. The principle here is that parental instruction should *always be clear*. As a parent, you need to sit down with your spouse (or a godly friend or church leader, if you are a single parent) to determine what sinful attitudes and actions warrant physical discipline. Thinking this through ahead of time will guard you from being the kind of parent who changes his or her mind like the wind. These instructions should then be consistently communicated to your children so that you do not unnecessarily provoke them to anger or discouragement.

> *Fathers, do not exasperate your children,*
> *so that they will not lose heart.*
> (Colossians 3:21)

Since this exhortation is directed at fathers, as is Ephesians 6:4, it seems clear that where there is a father in the home God expects him to take the lead in the discipline of the children. His word should be "the law of the home."

In our home, examples of offenses always worthy of discipline include deliberate disobedience or defiance of a clear and honorable command, lying, and disrespectful attitudes toward a parent or other authority figure. As a matter of principle we recommend that you *not* spank your child for violating instructions that you have not made clear *unless* the safety, or life, of the child or another is in danger. In other words, you should avoid spanking your child for doing something that you have not adequately defined as an offense.

When a first-time offense occurs, take time to explain to your child the reason his or her words, attitude, or behavior is sinful and what the consequence will be for a future occurrence. Accountability is thus established in the context of knowledge.

However, if a child runs onto a busy street, we personally believe we have one of those rare instances when we must apply the rod for the purpose of driving home the seriousness of the danger. Following this, a simple line may be established—a mark on the sidewalk or driveway, for example—to form a visual boundary over which the child may not cross. Explain to your toddler, "You may not go over this line. If you cross this line, Mommy or Daddy will need to discipline you." Children respond well to these simple boundaries because remaining within them enables them to cheerfully play as children, rather than feel the pressure of having to make decisions they are not yet wise enough to make.

Remember: Always be clear.

2. Maintain Self-Control

Parents who advocate the proper use of spanking as part of child-rearing should not be surprised when the world concludes that all forms are abusive since some parents are indeed guilty of taking their anger out on their children. Beware of this danger. The principle here is: *Never spank in anger.* Chastening your child when you are out of control is when you will come nearest to crossing the line of safety or opening a gate to the arena of abuse.

> Like a city that is broken into and without
> walls
> Is a man who has no control over his spirit.
> (Proverbs 25:28)

In addition, confusion is produced in the mind of a child when a parent who is out of control proceeds to correct the child for being out of control. This is hypocrisy. Dr. Martyn Lloyd-Jones rightly counseled, "When you are disciplining a child you should have first controlled yourself. If you try to discipline your child when you are in a temper, it is certain that you will do more harm than good. What right have you to say to your child that he needs discipline when you obviously need it yourself?"[10] We recommend that when you are angry, you instruct your child to go to his or her room to wait for you. This will give you ample time to "cool down" or go for a short walk in order to gain control of yourself and to pray to God for wisdom and grace to discipline properly.

Another practice that will help you overcome your own anger is to nip your child's sinful behavior in the bud, rather than tolerating it for hours, days, or weeks. By doing so you will prevent slow-burning frustration from building up inside you, which can easily turn into volcanic anger that will harm someone.

Remember: Never spank in anger.

3. Go to a Private Place

The goal of biblical discipline is correction, not humiliation. The principle here is: *Never spank in public.* Take the time to bring your child to a private place, usually taking his or her hand and walking there together. The goal must never be simply to disgrace the child in need of correction. This is based on the principle of Jesus's instruction to his disciples to confront one another in private.

> If your brother sins, go and show him his fault in private.
>
> (Matthew 18:15)

Though this Scripture addresses confrontation between believers within the local church, the principle of privacy may certainly be applied to correction in the home. Privacy shows respect for the child, guarding against the humiliation that often gives birth to resentment against one's parents.

Remember: Never spank in a public place.

4. Solicit a Confession

Having clearly communicated the behavioral standard, which has now been violated, maintained your self-control, and gone to a private place, it is time to solicit a confession from your child. Unless your child has a very sensitive conscience, knows he or she is in need of discipline, and comes to you admitting that need, you will need to put forth diligent effort toward gaining a humble confession of his or her wrongdoing.

Psalm 51 may very well be the most comprehensive description of confession that we find in the Bible. After pleading with God for grace and cleansing, David confesses that he knows what his sin is and he acknowledges it to God, who is chastening him:

> For I know my transgressions,
> And my sin is ever before me.
>
> (Psalm 51:3)

The principle here is: *Always be sure your child understands why he or she is being disciplined.* This is so important to the task of parenting! If we truly want God's richest blessing upon our children's lives, we must train them to acknowledge their own sin. Hidden, unconfessed sin will hinder that blessing from being experienced.

> He who conceals his transgressions will
>   not prosper,
> But he who confesses and forsakes them
>   will find compassion.
>
> (Proverbs 28:13)

Soliciting an honest, heartfelt confession from your child is best accomplished by asking questions, such as:

» What did you do that was wrong? Why does Mommy or Daddy need to discipline you?

» Is this sin?

» What does God think of sin?

» Did Jesus die for this sin?

Questions like these help the child to look beyond his or her wrong action, and the impending consequence, to his or her sin from God's perspective. We must help our children take full ownership of their sin so that we may gently lead them to the cross of Jesus, where they will find the grace, mercy, and cleansing their guilty consciences need. Addressing the child's heart, rather than merely the intellect, is the best means of stirring the conscience. This is best accomplished by asking questions like those above rather than voicing accusations.

Whenever possible, use simple and clear Scripture verses to expose the sin and provide instruction as to how we should correct our ways. This establishes God's Word as the ultimate authority in your home and turns any discipline session into an opportunity to communicate the gospel to our children.

> ... from childhood you have known the
> sacred writings which are able to give
> you the wisdom that leads to salvation
> through faith which is in Christ Jesus.
> All Scripture is inspired by God and
> profitable for teaching, for reproof, for
> correction, for training in righteousness;
> so that the man of God may be adequate,
> equipped for every good work.
>
> (2 Timothy 3:15–17)

By leading our children to confession we aim to help them experience the cleansing power of true forgiveness. The word "confess" means "to say the same thing." It means to agree with God that one's action or attitude is as sinful as God declares it to be. True confession says, "God, the judgment you pronounce upon my sin is accurate. I am guilty." Therefore, confession says to the person we've wronged, "I was wrong when I did, or said, *this* to you [get specific]. Will you please forgive me?" It does not merely say, "I am sorry. I apologize."

An apology is an expression of regret that does not always communicate admission of one's own guilt. It may convey "I feel bad" but not necessarily "I was wrong." An apology is what we offer when we accidentally step on someone's foot. A confession, on the other hand, is what we offer when we have actually sinned against another person. By asking "Will you please forgive me?" we not only own up to our sin, but we also give the offended party an opportunity to display the grace of forgiveness toward us by replying, "I forgive you."

For biblical discipline to be most effective at reaching the heart of our child, we need to take time to solicit a confession before using the rod, so that our child's mind is confronted with truth and he or she is thus given the opportunity to have his or her conscience made clean through true confession and gracious forgiveness. This principle will be taught at different levels depending on the child's age. However, its foundational truth must begin to be laid in the younger years.[11]

Remember: Always be sure your child understands why he or she is being disciplined.

5. Apply a Neutral Tool to the Appropriate Area

We strongly recommend the use of a neutral tool for spanking, rather than your hand, but again stress that the neutral tool is *never* to be used in anger or to abuse. Hands are for expressing tenderness and affection, not inflicting pain. There is something inherently grievous when a child cringes and backs away from his or her parent when an expression of affection is offered. Parents should never slap their child's face, strike him or her across the head, or shake their child.[12] These are all examples of abuse. The principle we need to apply here is this: *Never spank any part of the body other than the rump.*

In our house, we refer to this neutral tool as "the wisdom paddle" because of its purpose of driving away foolishness and implanting wisdom (Proverbs 22:15). The only exception to this rod-only practice in our home is a quick slap on the hand of a very young child, usually at the crawling stage, who needs to feel slight pain immediately connected to the act of disobedience. Young children do not easily understand time factors so it is important for the chastisement to take place as soon as possible following the offense.

The biblical basis for our conviction to not use our hands to spank is the regularity of the use of the word "rod" in the book of Proverbs (it is used a total of nine times). All but one of these uses are clear references to some form of correction.[13]

Three of the remaining eight uses refer to the foolish person who lacks understanding and is, therefore, in need of wisdom (10:13; 14:3; 26:3). This is certainly true of children as well. Five occurrences of "the rod" specifically mention the physical discipline of children.

» "He who withholds his *rod* hates his son, but he who loves him disciplines him diligently" (13:24).

» "Foolishness is bound up in the heart of a child; the *rod* of discipline will remove it far from him" (22:15).

» "Do not hold back discipline from the child, although you strike him with the *rod*, he will not die. You shall strike him with the *rod* and rescue his soul from Sheol" (23:13–14).

» "The *rod* and reproof give wisdom, but a child who gets his own way brings shame to his mother" (29:15).

The rump, or buttocks, is the part of the body that appears to be designed by God for this form of discipline. It contains no bones that can be broken or brains that could be damaged, but does contain an ample supply of tender flesh that readily feels pain. When properly applied the pain of the rod becomes a deterrent to continued foolishness.

Remember: Never spank any part of the body other than the rump.

6. Do Not Allow Angry Crying or Screaming

The key word is *angry*. The proper application of the rod will produce some crying (if you have carried out Law 5 properly), but you must not tolerate angry crying, which usually evidences a lack of submission to the parent as well as to the discipline process. The sorrow of true remorse is what will be most beneficial to your child. If after applying the rod to the appropriate area your child jumps or screams or shakes his or her fists at you, it is obvious that your discipline has not effectively reached your child's conscience. The principle here is: *Always seek brokenness.*

A humble spirit and a contrite heart are essential responses to biblical discipline. This is evident in God's chastisement of King David when, intent on correcting and restoring the disobedient king, the Lord successfully applied discipline toward the goal of producing a humble spirit.

The sacrifices of God are a broken spirit;

*A broken and a contrite heart, O God, You
will not despise.*

(Psalm 51:17)

While children are very young we must
sometimes say to them after the use of the rod,
"You may cry, but you may not scream. You may
cry, but you may not throw a fit." It is important
to teach your children to submit to your discipline
rather than resist it. This will prepare them to
submit to God's discipline later in life rather than
stiffen their necks against him (Hebrews 12:11).
Consistently ask the Lord to use you as a tool to
bring your child to this blessed state of true sorrow
and humble brokenness.

Remember: Always seek brokenness.

7. Seal the Reconciliation with Affection and Prayer

As stated in the previous chapter, Ephesians 6:4
instructs us to "bring up" our children in the
discipline and instruction of the Lord. Wrapped
in this exhortation is the element of tenderness.
Therefore, the principle here is: *Always end the
discipline session with expressions of love.* Let your
children cry on your shoulder. Let them express

their sorrow. Let there be lots of hugs. Don't ever discipline them and then cast them away into isolation. The common practice of "time-outs" is unbiblical because it encourages isolation rather than restoration. Biblical discipline always seeks to restore, to bring the disobedient one back to fellowship with the one who has been sinned against.

Prayer is also important—on the part of both parent and child (if he or she is old enough to verbalize). When God disciplined David, the guilty king confessed his sin to God in prayer:

> *Against You, You only, I have sinned*
> *And done what is evil in Your sight.*
> (*Psalm 51:4*)

It is essential for our children to understand that they have not merely sinned against us (or perhaps also against a sibling or another child), but first and foremost they have sinned against a holy God.

» First, the child should confess the specific sin to God. When children are very young they will need your help. "Dear Lord, please forgive me for ..." Confession begins to instill the fear of the Lord in your child, which is the beginning of wisdom (Psalm 111:10).

» Second, the parent who carries out the correction should pray with, and for, the child. Thank God for the child by name and for his or her willingness to learn from discipline. Pray for the child to grow in obedience (name the specific area, especially if it is a repetitive sin). Thank God for the forgiveness that he provides because of the death and resurrection of Jesus.

» Third, after prayer, ask the child, "What will you do next time?" This will prepare him or her to respond obediently the next time he or she faces the same test.

» Fourth, the child should confess his or her sin to those he or she has wronged and ask for their forgiveness. Teach your child to ask for forgiveness by saying something like, "I hurt you. Will you please forgive me?" rather than merely, "I'm sorry." Remember, an apology does not equal confession if there is no admission of wrongdoing and subsequent request for forgiveness.

Remember: Always end the discipline session with expressions of love.

These seven principles, when faithfully applied to the correction of our children's disobedience, will instill in them a healthy fear of the Lord, sensitivity to sin, respect for authority, and appreciation for the grace of forgiveness found only in Jesus Christ.

FROM ONE MOM TO ANOTHER

My four-year old daughter was once helping me make pizza dough in the kitchen. As I began putting on the toppings, I became distracted, but then noticed she had gotten a dishcloth out of the drawer and had gone into the dining room. I was curious, but did not take the time to see what she was doing until I heard my husband say, "We have a problem here."

I poked my head around the corner to see her wiping up white flour from the hardwood floor and the area rug. When I asked her what had happened, she explained that she was "making it rain in the house." I could have disciplined her for making such a mess, but realized this was a moment of childishness, not disobedience or defiance. Therefore, instead of applying the rod, I took the time to instruct her. I then explained what the consequences would be if she were to "make it rain in the house" again. Then we cleaned up the dusty mess together.

Conclusion

When God appointed Abraham to be the father of his chosen nation, he revealed his divine will:

> For I have chosen him, so that he may command his children and his household after him to keep the way of the LORD by doing righteousness and justice.
>
> (Genesis 18:19)

The term "command" highlights the delegation of God's authority to Abraham for the purpose of training his children to know God and to practice righteousness. This is the task of godly parenting.

Children are valuable to God. They are his property—loaned to parents for a short season. Since they are on loan to us there is a day coming when we will give an account to the Creator for our stewardship. For this reason it seems utterly preposterous for parents to raise their children apart from a conscious attempt to understand and apply the directions given to us by God in the Bible. The purpose of this booklet has been to lay this biblical framework in a brief manner in order to help parents comprehend their divinely delegated authority and to provide practical wisdom in the application of that authority to the discipline and training of their children to the end that they may know and love God.

Parents, we stand in the gap between our children and God. We are God's first and preferred avenue of reaching our children's hearts so that they may develop biblical faith and godly character which flow from a healthy fear of God and an accurate knowledge of the gospel of his salvation. May we learn to depend upon his grace for each new day as we strive to be faithful to our task!

Personal Application Projects

You will need some blank note sheets, or pages in your journal, to respond to the following questions in a way that will prove most beneficial.

1. (a) According to the Bible, children possess two fundamental duties: to listen to their parents in order to obey them, and to demonstrate honor and respect.

   Look up the following Scriptures and note what each command entails:

   Colossians 3:20; Ephesians 6:1; Proverbs 1:8; Proverbs 13:1; Proverbs 15:5.

   (b) Look up the following Scriptures. Note the reasons children must be trained to listen to and obey their parents.

   Proverbs 15:5; Proverbs 6:2–22; Ephesians 6:2–3; Proverbs 3:1–2; Proverbs 4:20–22; Proverbs 2:1–5.

(c) Look up the following Scriptures. Note the reasons children must be trained to respect and honor their parents.

Exodus 20:12; Exodus 21:15; Leviticus 19:3; 1 Samuel 15:23; Proverbs 19:26; Proverbs 20:20; Proverbs 29:15; Proverbs 30:11–14; Proverbs 30:17.

2. Read Luke 6:45. List some fruits of heart attitudes mentioned by Jesus in this verse. Why is it important for parents to hold their children accountable for their attitudes? Should disrespectful attitudes in children be grounds for discipline? Explain.

3. Read Hebrews 12:3–11. Answer the following questions.

(a) Discipline flows from which commitment (v. 5)?

(b) How does the absence of discipline feed insecurity in the relationship (vv. 7–8)?

(c) What are the proper goals of discipline (v. 10)?

(d) Why must discipline be painful (v. 11a)?

(e) What benefit does discipline bring to the one who learns to submit to it (v. 11b)?

4. Review the Scriptures used throughout this booklet. Make a list of five verses that you will commit *yourself* to memorize. We suggest you begin with Proverbs 13:24.

5. Review the Scriptures mentioned in this booklet. Make a list of five verses that you will teach *your child* to memorize. We recommend you begin with Ephesians 6:1.

6. Write a one-page prayer to the Lord. Thank him for the children he has blessed you with. Confess any sin you may be guilty of as a parent. Ask for his wisdom and help. Commit yourself to applying to your parenting task the biblical principles you have learned.

7. Write each of your children's names on the top of a separate 3 x 5 card. List at least three attitude and/or behavior changes you desire to see the Lord make in your child this year. Use these cards to help you pray for your children each day. Above all, pray that the Holy Spirit will use your parental discipline and instruction to bring your child to genuine faith in Christ as Lord and Savior.

Where Can I Get More Help?

The following books will prove beneficial to any parent who wishes to establish a biblical philosophy of parenting.

Decker, Barbara, *Proverbs for Parenting* (Boise, ID: Lynn's Bookshelf, 1989)

Fabrizio, Pat, *Under Loving Command* (Cupertino, CA: Dime, 1969)

Farley, William P., *Gospel-Powered Parenting* (Phillipsburg, NJ: P&R, 2009)

Kostenberger, Andreas J., *God, Marriage, and Family* (Wheaton, IL: Crossway, 2004)

Lessin, Roy, *Spanking: Why, When, How?* (Ada, MI: Bethany House, 1982)

MacArthur, John F., *What the Bible Says About Parenting* (Nashville: Word, 2000)

Mack, Wayne, *Your Family God's Way* (Phillipsburg, NJ: P&R, 1991)

Priolo, Lou, *Teach Them Diligently* (Woodruff, SC: Timeless Texts, 2000)

Ray, Bruce, *Withhold Not Correction* (Phillipsburg, NJ: P&R, 1978)

Tripp, Paul David, *Age of Opportunity* (Phillipsburg, NJ: P&R, 2001)

Tripp, Tedd, *Shepherding a Child's Heart* (Wapwallopen, PA: Shepherd Press, 1995)

—and Margy, *Instructing a Child's Heart* (Wapwallopen, PA: Shepherd Press, 2008)

END NOTES

1   These are fictitious names, though based upon a true story.
2   Martha Irvine, in The Sheboygan Press, June 18, 2002.
3   Jim Newheiser, Opening Up Proverbs (Leominster: Day One, 2008), 151.
4   Temper Tantrums: A Normal Part of Growing Up (Elk Grove, IL: American Academy of Pediatrics, 1989).
5   Emphasis in all Scripture verses is the authors'.
6   The Old Testament term Sheol most often refers to the grave (Genesis 37:35; 1 Samuel 2:6), but in some instances it refers to hell, the abode of the wicked dead (Psalm 9:17; Proverbs 23:14).
7   Pat Fabrizio, Under Loving Command (Cupertino, CA: Dime, 1969), 10.
8   Richard C. Trench, Synonyms of the New Testament (Grand Rapids, MI: Baker, 1989), 126–127.
9   Fritz Rienecker & Cleon Rogers, Linguistic Key to the Greek New Testament (Grand Rapids, MI: Zondervan, 1976), 540.
10 D. Martyn Lloyd Jones, Life in the Spirit in Marriage, Home & Work (Grand Rapids, MI: Baker, 1973), 279.

11 To gain a better understanding of the importance of true confession we highly recommend that every parent read the article "True Stories: A Tale of Two Confessions" by Ken Sande, found at the website of Peacemaker Ministries: http://www.peacemaker.net/.

12 Shaking a child, especially an infant, may cause brain damage.

13 Proverbs 22:8 says, "He who sows iniquity will reap vanity, and the rod of his fury will perish." This speaks of the diminishing power of the wicked ruler "to discharge his anger and advance his self-centered agenda at the expense of the unsuspecting and undefended" (John A. Kitchen, Proverbs [Mentor Commentary; Fearn: Christian Focus, 2006], 498).

BOOKS IN THE HELP! SERIES INCLUDE...

Help! He's Struggling with Pornography
  ISBN 978-1-63342-003-8

Help! Someone I Love Has Been Abused
  ISBN 978-1-63342-006-9

Help! Someone I Love Has Cancer
  ISBN 978-1-63342-012-0

Help! I Want to Change
  ISBN 978-1-63342-015-1

Help! My Spouse Has Been Unfaithful
  ISBN 978-1-63342-018-2

Help! My Baby Has Died
  ISBN 978-1-63342-021-2

Help! I Have Breast Cancer
  ISBN 978-1-63342-024-3

Help! I'm a Slave to Food
  978-1-63342-027-4

Help! My Teen Struggles With Same-Sex Attractions
  ISBN 978-1-63342-030-4

Help! She's Struggling With Pornography
  ISBN 978-1-63342-033-5

Help! I Can't Get Motivated
  ISBN 978-1-63342-036-6

Help! I'm a Single Mom
  ISBN 978-1-63342-039-7

Help! I'm Confused About Dating
  ISBN 978-1-63342-042-7

Help! I'm Drowning in Debt
  ISBN 978-1-63342-045-8

Help! My Teen is Rebellious
  ISBN 978-1-63342-048-9

Help! I'm Depressed
  ISBN 978-1-63342-051-9

Help! I'm Living With Terminal Illness
  ISBN 978-1-63342-054-0

Help! I Feel Ashamed
  ISBN 978-1-63342-057-1

Help! I Can't Submit to My Husband
  ISBN 978-1-63342-060-1

Help! Someone I Love Has Alzheimers
  ISBN 978-1-63342-063-2

Help! I Can't Handle All These Trials
  ISBN 978-1-63342-066-3

Help! I Can't Forgive
  ISBN 978-1-63342-069-4

Help! My Anger is Out of Control
  ISBN 978-1-63342-072-4

Help! My Friend is Suicidal
  ISBN 978-1-63342-075-5

Help! I'm in a Conflict
  ISBN 978-1-63342-078-6

Help! I Need a Good Church
  ISBN 978-1-63342-081-6

(More titles in preparation)